HEAVY IS THE HEAD

sumaya enyegue

central
avenue

2023

Trigger warning:
This book deals with topics of sexual assault, violence against
bipoc, and struggles with mental health.
Please take care.

Published by Central Avenue Poetry, an imprint of Central Avenue Marketing Ltd.
www.centralavenuepublishing.com

HEAVY IS THE HEAD

Trade Paperback: 978-1-77168-297-8
EPUB: 978-1-77168-298-5

Published in Canada
Printed in United States of America

1. POETRY / African   2. POETRY / American/African American & Black

1 3 5 7 9 10 8 6 4 2

For every hand that has held me with tenderness:
my parents, my family, my friends.

heavy is the head

GIRLHOOD

the goal is for us to grow up, right?
boys morph into men and girls into
gaping wounds.
do you know what it's like to be born an adult?
to go from fetus to woman?
when you can't afford the luxury of childhood,
your innocence is an afterthought.

if you're going to tell me anything, then
tell me about the sun.
tell me about how it rises each morning
—in spite of us, regardless of whether we
want it to or not.

tell me about the girls, especially the ones
that didn't survive the night.
give me their names.
let me cradle them in my palms.
let me write them down with all the others.

tell me about the fights and the arguments,
about how there's bad blood now.
tell me about the bad blood and I will tell
you that there's
no such thing as good blood.
only thick blood.
only blood that's forced to stay—only
gaping wounds.

REARRANGING MY TRAUMAS

the anagram for skin is sink / isn't that funny? / how black bodies tossed from slave ships sunk to the bottom / of the Dead Sea / poured directly into the wound.

the anagram for negro is goner / as in gone / as in vanished without a whisper of how / half-forgotten / dressed in scars and bullet holes / and called / couture.

the anagram for burned is burden / the smell of smoke / a memory that hasn't turned to ash / if you saw me / all brown skin and inferno eyes / next to a blackened corpse / would you be able to tell the difference?

the anagram of rape is reap / that which he did not sow / the body is the temple / he came to absolve himself of sin / left tiny tortures on the carpet / I am still picking them up.

the anagram for hatred is thread / I am hanging / dangling / between the fine line of / resentment / and loving you in reverse.

DARK (SKIN) HUMOR

Black girl walks into a room. She is instantly the joke. Always is. Everyone
laughs. Points fingers. What a sight she is. She is a beacon for everything that
will cause her pain. Men hit on black girl. Men hit black girl. Men hit and call
it a   punch line. Black girl shrinks. Makes herself smaller. They find
her anyway. Ogle her skin. Her hair. Her body. They are laughing but they are
fascinated. They want what black girl has but still want black girl silent. But
black girl is strong, right? Always is. Always has to be. No one believes black
girl has depression or other myths. Black girl must provide. Black girl must
abandon her mother tongue on a shelf and train her mouth to be sophisticated.
To be less ugly. Less native. Black girl is either too black, or not black enough.
Black girl must fight. And fight. And lose. Black girl must write poetry so
other black girls can relate. She must dim her anger so that no one is afraid of
her. Black girl is tired. She always is. But she has to laugh. She must giggle with
everyone or else she is ruining the fun for the whole group. So black girl does.
She bites her tongue and laughs.

IS IT STILL SEASONAL DEPRESSION IF IT HAPPENS ALL YEAR ROUND?

Every night I google symptoms of depression to remind
myself that someone out there has given this feeling a
name, has translated this emptiness into a language I can
speak.
My sister tells me I'll feel better if I cry but what good
is salt and water when I have been drowning for months.
I am a sponge for everyone's misery but my own.
This diagnosis is too fickle a word: it breaks on my tongue every time
I try to say it out loud.
I tell my family what the psychiatrist said and they immediately
start building me a new spine—one that can carry the weight of new burdens.

will I survive myself?

Every antidepressant that melts on my tongue is just another way
to keep track of the time.
It's finally spring. This time, there will be flowers, yet not a funeral in sight.
This time,

death is afraid of me.

"HOW LUCKY ARE YOU? YOU GET TO BE VIOLATED BY STRANGE MEN AND LIVE TO TELL THE TALE."

- and so, i think about how i was catcalled at 14 by a man who looked all too familiar so i ran home to my father and cried in his lap: i became a woman and then morphed back into a little girl for two different men like some sick magic trick.

- once, i peeled back my skin to count my bones and i didn't like all the flesh i saw—all the proof that i was in fact exactly like my mother in all the wrong ways.

- i have not lived long enough to be deemed a war hero but my God i have suffered, i have lost,   i have screamed,   i have used my body as a weapon and it has not made me worthy of a medal   of a parade   of a standing ovation as i walk across the stage. i just want someone to recognize that this is not easy, that this is not how i imagined it would be.

- even here, in the crevices of this poem, i am still running.

CONFESSIONS OF A BEAST

Okay, fine. I'll admit it: I'm not doing okay. I'm *not* fine. Things *could* be better. What now? Now that I've confessed that I am falling apart, what will you do? How will you pull me out of the labyrinth? Were you lying when you said you would love me at my worst? I only ask because the worst is here and it's going to stay for a while. I am not a monster. I only snarl when provoked. I haven't hidden under a bed in years, I promise. It's not my fault people are scared of me. I never meant to hurt anyone. I just wanted to be beautiful. I just wanted to be human—whichever came first. I can use my hands for good if I'm given the chance. I can resurrect the dead versions of myself if given enough notice. You carry a palm full of *almosts* and have me eating out of your hands. And it *almost* looks as though you love me, but you flinch every time I touch you. You trip over my name like you can't recognize me anymore. I'm still beautiful and I'm still yours. Please believe me. Please believe me. Please bel—

INSTRUCTIONS FOR LOVING YOUR FRIENDS

1. Tell your friends you love them. Make them believe you. Turn them into family or a ballad or a pinky promise well-kept. Give them your heart, have them wrap it in gauze so it doesn't turn septic.

2. Laugh at their jokes, even the ones that aren't funny, especially the bad puns.

3. Remind them to unclench their jaws, to loosen their grip on realities that do not serve them.

4. Be their shelter, write them poems, read it to them out loud.

5. Take bad pictures of them then post them on their birthdays. Tell them they have never looked more beautiful than they do right now, than they have ever given themselves credit for.

6. Make fun of their taste in music then memorize the lyrics to their favorite song so you can sing it in the car with them.

7. Watch them cry, give them your silence. When the sobs stop: tell them there's nothing to worry about, that there's no burden they can't share with you.

8. Tell them that all good, clean love begins with sacrifice—that they have made the ultimate one.

THE SUMMER OF GOODBYES

The summer of '06 was spent with limbs I had not yet grown
into and a smile not yet ruined by ghosts. I was happy and the sun
was forgiving. There wasn't a pavement my knees had not kissed and
there wasn't a streetlamp that didn't whisper my name.
I never grew tired of dawn and didn't shudder at the thought of closing my eyes.
There was always a song to be sung and a dance to make
my body liquid. Cities burned and buildings fell but I made
castles out of the ruins and called anywhere I could
rest my head for a moment a home.

The summer of '07, I swallowed gum and my brother
told me I would die. I spent an hour crying then said goodbye to all my
toys and gave my dad instructions on how to take care of them.
I rested my head on the pavement my knees once kissed
and deemed it the perfect final resting place.
My mom woke me up 20 minutes later and scolded
my brother for playing such a cruel prank.

I wonder if someday I will find the perfect final resting
place and if I'll cry before I do. Will I say goodbye and give instructions
on how to take care of the things I love, and will the streetlamps
scream my name in mourning?
Will the pavements remember the knees that remained
tender against the harsh finality of gravel?
Will my mother wake me up and tell me it's a
sick joke or will I finally grow into my limbs and rest with the ghost of a smile?

AM I NEXT?

This poem isn't meant to be a sugar-coated bullet that enters you lightly.
It's meant to rip through your skin and enter your flesh
unwelcomed because like all difficult things, it's painful to talk about.

They created another rape helpline last week:
the last two were at capacity.

Another girl called today.
Said she can't find her body.
Said she thinks her rapist took it with him.

Another girl died today.
I watched her body turn to dust
Helped her bury her trust in men.

We have watched the media console and defend the
perpetrator but never the victim.
They have measured the length of skirts
but never the number of tears she cried.

To defend a rapist, is to see something of yourself in them.
To doubt women, is to see nothing remotely human in them.

LOST CREATURE

If you must remember anything, remember this: There used to
be a place I could go to forget.
Call it a feeling
or a home,
or a box with your name on it—it was there.
I would crawl into this space and suddenly I could peel
back the sun and dismantle my misery with the snap of my finger.
That place is gone now. Vanished. I click my heels together and
nothing happens. Now I am stuck here, in this body—with these
hands. And it's exhausting to think about what these palms will
do if I let them, if I don't tie them behind my back so they don't
reach for the things that bruise in the night. Or perhaps I assign
too much responsibility on this body beyond being a circuit of tissue
and bone. Meaning, is my heart really a bloodthirsty creature captured
behind a steel rib cage or is the hammering in my ears just the price
I pay for being an ongoing outline of breathing? Is it possible that my
hands are just my hands and not orchestrators of the wreckage?

MISSING PERSONS REPORT

I woke up one morning and breathed a
sigh of relief that it was a bad dream,
that there was no way I had his heavy body
holding mine down, that my screams were
just a figment of my imagination.
So, imagine my surprise when I looked in the
mirror and realized my body was nowhere to be found.
The police officer I filed the missing body's report with asks,
What were you wearing when you last saw it?
Don't you know that fifteen-year-old bodies are all the
rage with grown men these days?

I looked everywhere.
Checked my last known address.
Blamed myself for being so careless.
So naive. Everyone pitied the poor girl
with no body. *How will she ever recover*
from such a violent robbery?

When I got the call that they'd found a fresh
corpse that fit my description, I went down
to the station to identify my remains. I could barely
recognize my own body. *We found the thief*
trying to bury your bones in his backyard, the police officer said.
He just couldn't help himself.

IN THE NAME OF LOVE

I am no saint   only flesh and bone   only clumsy hands and   big heart with nowhere to put it, so I place it in your palms   and you return it   broken and mangled   and tell me *all the kids are doing it these days*   that everyone is aching   that it's fashionable to throb all alone in the dark. I am sick   with the shame of my wanting,   bloated with the possibility of belonging to something that doesn't ruin me   or give me sharp edges   which I keep using to stab the soft parts that   remain. When will I learn that I am nothing more than a network of pulsatile grief.   I am my best kept secret— I do not even know myself. I could be walking down the street and I still wouldn't know   whose ghost I belong to. All I know is that my heart is still scattered all over the dirty floor but I manage to love   you with the cleanest parts of it.

METAMORPHISM

Without giving it a name, what do you call the first
punishment? I mean, how would you even know
you're bleeding if you've never hemorrhaged?
Never clotted   under a harsh light? Do you know
you're an animal? Or has language made you soft
enough to believe your teeth aren't fangs, that your
hands cannot damage? You carry so much violence
in your belly, it's a marvel how you haven't vomited all
over the good furniture. You are dilating with fresh grief,
you are howling into your pillow; you are calling your
~~abuser~~ lover ~~messiah~~ again. You are abbreviating back
into a calf—smothered in your mother's sacrifice like you
have nothing to be sorry about. Everyone is innocent until
they are handed a butcher's knife. Every newborn is presumed
dead until they cry and suddenly you clot like the creature you are,
but you seem to forget that not even blood is thicker than regret.

IS THIS THE LIFE YOU WANTED?

If I could choose between this life and the one I thought I would have, I would eliminate the choice altogether. What I've got is what I've got   and no amount of wishing is going to stop the world from catching fire so it doesn't matter if I ignite in my bedroom or go up in flames in yours— I'm still burning all the same. I'm still blackened earth and dead eyes. If I could choose between love and grief, I would eliminate the choice altogether because knowing you is love but loving you is   grief so I keep going around in circles trying to convince myself that this was all worth it   that I chose correctly   that you were the best decision I ever made even when you keep making a liar out of me.

I'M TIRED OF BEING LOVED ONLY IN THEORY

There it is again—that sound.
Footsteps towards an exit, bones
popping back into place, the violent
bruising of a delicate throat. We can turn
anything into a song if we are sad enough.
Were you lying when you said you would still
be here in the morning? Because dawn is
breathing down the napes of our necks but I can
feel you leaving the bed. I just want to be clean
enough to hold, to be good enough to experience
for more than a day. I am tired of being loved
without the burden of proof, without a stitch of
evidence. I am so sick of being a clean slate for
everyone's wanting, a palate cleanser before your
fairy-tale ending. For once, can I be the final destination,
the trembling hand at the deathbed, the last thing lingering
in your palms before you rinse them clean?

EXCERPTS OF CONVERSATIONS I WILL HAVE WITH MY DAUGHTER

1. Stop walking like an apology. You don't have to be sorry you exist so loudly, so unabashedly.
2. There are days where you will be shaped like a question mark—uncertain of how you can keep yourself afloat in a house built on water.
3. There is no glass ceiling for you to break, only shards of broken systems—tread lightly.
4. People will hurt you and then leave—you must pretend that this is normal.
5. Sometimes rage is the only thing you can hold safely in your mouth—sometimes it tastes a little bit like love.
6. Someday you will learn how to turn off the hurt, how to dim the ache. It just takes a bit of practice.

CONFESSIONS II

To answer your question, yes—if I could, I would split
the memory of you in half and only keep the bits that don't have teeth.
Why is everyone I love so fluid? How do they slip
through my fingers no matter how tightly I close my fists?
Admitting I'm sad feels like a betrayal to all the things I once survived,
everything I once outlasted.
Everything I've ever called beautiful is now
collateral damage. I mean, am I actually real if I have not
bled in your hands? I mean, sometimes even
blood is not a good enough reason to stay.

DID OUR FATHERS INVENT SILENCE OR IS THAT WHAT MAKES THEM OUR FATHERS?

after safia elhillo

Forgiveness comes in the shape of a two-way street and I'm the only one on the road for miles. I gave myself my father's face so I could recognize an illusion when I see one. Everyone I love is not here and by that I mean holding my hand. Everyone I love is dead and by that I mean my anxiety has taken over again. I am brimming with shame and it makes my skin glisten. I am easier to love when you turn off the quiet. I am easier to hold when I don't have another poem or song in my mouth. I am so used to having unwanted language in my throat, I never stopped to think about what would happen when I had nothing left to say. After all, what is silence if not my father staring back at me with a face like my own.

HOW I CHOOSE TO DIE

a mortal deity / with a handful of teeth / by old wounds bursting at the seams
/ when the healing takes a smoke break / in therapy / when i have no more
poems to spare / after i eulogize each sharp misery / before i resurrect each
blunt heartache / after i reconcile with my hijab / when i stitch my lungs
back together during the autopsy / whilst i watch you go up in flames / as my
consent is snatched from my frigid hands / after i teach the ocean full of girls
how to become liquid / before i get called outside of my name / when I drink
the gallon of the venom i keep tucked in my vein / when the bullet comes
knocking to collect its debt / during the hymen inspection / by opening the
lion's cage and welcoming the carbon copy of my imprisoned kin home /
without your name tugging at my wrist.

ORIGIN STORY

I think home could no longer stand the taste of me.
I, all cocoa-skinned and bad knees
with velvet eyes and a maze of hair.
My blood is acidic and my village couldn't
bear to keep that which
ruins the soil.
Mother was pregnant with me when we fled,
as if home could sense my looming presence.
I take up too much room
with my appetite for that which breaks me over and over again.
I was born to be human: to be black girl and safe. Can you imagine that? Safe.
I was birthed to be someone,
not a headline.
Someday I'll get to go home:
when I have mastered the art of not wearing grief so easily.
My grandmother will cup my face in her weathered hands and search my face
for the betrayal of sadness.
Satisfied, she will wrap me in the belly of her arms and I
will be born again.

AFRICAN IDIOMS I KEEP TUCKED UNDER MY TONGUE

There is a saying in my culture,
"However fast a man, he will not outrun his own shadow."
Which is to say,
one cannot run from their own darkness.
We are born with something and it is our duty
to endure it no matter how long it takes the
blood to dry.

There is a saying in my culture,
"It is the pot that boils but the dish that gets all the credit."
Which is to say,
she crucifies herself on the cross
only for him to be called the savior.
She removes the knife from her back
and the person who put it there faints
from the blood loss.

There is a saying in my culture,
"Beauty is an empty calabash."
Which is to say,
vanity makes one hollow.
Fill your body with jewels
and risk losing a heart of gold.

APPENDECTOMY

We used to have what it takes. Gosh, do you remember that? There wasn't a light harsh enough to blind us. Now we have diluted our desires to be tepid enough to swim in. We did everything right—placed our trust in each other's palms and died on every hill we could name. I would burn down entire cities if it meant keeping you warm. I lie and tell myself you would do the same. If you carry heartbreak long enough it transforms an organ, a throbbing appendix. And perhaps it's stupid of me to compare you to an organ but you too were a visceral part of me, a body part I didn't really need, something I could live without. But how do I cut you out of me? How much pain is necessary? It was never like you to let the incision heal.

[WHEN A BLACK GIRL DIES, THE LAST THING TO DECOMPOSE IS HER HEART.]

There are moments when I forget I am not wanted and then someone
calls me a nigger and the memory slaps me awake. I have been brown
for a thousand lifetimes and yet the violence of this skin still surprises
me—how it can bruise so easily and still keep the scars hidden. And
I could write you an ocean of poems about how I was taught that you
could be black or you could be beautiful, but you couldn't be both.
Why can't I be both?

GIRLHOOD, PT. 2

I feel most woman when I'm bleeding all over the carpet. There is nothing I know better than to blend in with the scenery, than to make violence tender.

At my last dentist appointment, I had two molars ripped from my mouth and I was disappointed to see that my teeth were not as sharp as I needed them to be. The pain in my mouth lasted three pills (it's the only way I know how to measure healing).

I feel most girl when I am being humiliated, when my body glows with shame. It's when I look the prettiest, I think. This body has known nothing but blunt dissection. I would name every bit of this gross anatomy if I could, if it would help. But giving my mouth a Latin name isn't going to change the way it smiles.

Give me three days and I will come back pure. Give me three days and I can make this body less horrific. I can make you forget why you were disgusted in the first place. Give me three days and the carpet will be as good as new. Give me three days and you won't even know I'm here.

DISPOSABLE

When it comes down to it, even love is not a strong enough illusion to keep you soft. You will clot like granite, and when the day comes that you have to look a self-appointed god in the eye, you will tell them you cannot worship them without stuttering. What exactly about me angers you the most? Is it that I am both black and alive? Two crimes existing simultaneously. I would peel off this skin and keep it somewhere safe if I could. But every morning I have to wake up and do my best impression of a moving target and hope I make it home in one piece. Because when it comes down to it, even blackness is not a strong enough illusion to keep you safe.

LOVE CARRIES VIOLENCE ON ITS BACK

As in, a rose is not a rose without its thorns. As in, my first love unhinged their jaw and swallowed my youth before I could remember it fondly.

As in, you carved a heart before plunging the knife into my chest.

As in, if I could point to where it hurt I would have a map of every location you kissed me and meant it.

As in, everything comes at a price: some of us just pay with grief with blood with the skin of our teeth. You're so used to mistaking me for a corpse that you forgot to uncross your fingers when you told me that this was forever. You're so used to treating me like shit that you forgot I was once something you wanted.

GOOD DAUGHTERS

Have you learnt nothing? Good girls don't end up on the news. Only rotten ones. Only the ones who ask for it—their pretty smiles forever immortalized on the silver screen while their bodies collect dust in the ditch they were left in. Their mothers knew this day would come—they just didn't know when. Daughters invented love and then loved nothing but made sure to come back home every night. Their brothers invented regret and yet apologize for nothing except the things that leave a scar. *But why didn't you say anything?* This silence is a cyanide pill stuck in my throat—I'll die if I open my mouth and I am doomed if I swallow. I just can't seem to spit it out.

PEACHES

she lies through her teeth at every doctor's appointment / says she fell / says she walked into the wall / silly her / so clumsy / the doctor mends her bones twice a month / and she mends her heart twice as much / she drives home / tells herself to stop being so clumsy / begs herself to stop falling / to stop falling / one day she's going to run into that wall / and disappear / this wall has arms / and a baritone voice / this wall doesn't take no for an answer / the wall convinces her that it's her only shelter / calls her peaches / she bruises so easily / all pink and pretty / eats her alive / leaves nothing but the pit / of her stomach / yes, it takes strength to leave / but goodness, can you imagine what it takes to stay?

GIRLHOOD, PT. 3

The word you are looking for is girl: lost girl   dead girl   girl oozing of misery
endangered species   shiny object   poor thing   dead thing. I will use the word
girl as many times as it takes for you to believe me.

Alone is the safest I've ever been.

No one has marked me as theirs—yet. But what good is a girl if no one
humiliates her? What else does *girl* have to lose if not more blood, if not more
of her youth. To be born ~~victim~~ girl is to run before anyone chases you. I am
both girl and woman: girl when my body is not my own, woman when my
body is not my own. My body is not my own.

I'M AFRAID OF EVERYTHING THAT WANTS ME

It turns out you were wrong about me. I *can* beg for things other than love: like a warm hand to hold, like the blunt knife of yearning, like a soft place to land. Yes, I know these are just different words for love but let's not get hung up on the semantics. The point is that I have my father's face but my mother's anger so I throw rocks through windows I can see my reflection in. The point is, nothing worth keeping has ever wanted me back. The point is, my little sister tells me she wants to be like me when she grows up and my instinct is to apologize. I have mistakenly made this look like a life worth living when it is just endless giving. *The point is*—the only thing I miss is your hands because they are the only proof I have that I can be touched. How do I translate ache into a language I can speak? I don't know how to pour myself into tomorrow without writing off today as a close call. I want a love that doesn't hurt too much, only a little, only enough to warn me. I am sick of being an unwanted thing—I have never been anything else. I have never looked like someone deserving of a soft place to land.

MY PHONE AUTOCORRECTS MY NAME TO SUMMER

Summer chooses violence, scorches everything that touches the pavement.
Everyone wants *Summer* for a month but soon grows sick of the heat, the
humidity, they retreat back into their homes, turn on the air conditioning and
wait for winter. But this *Summer* is endless this *Summer* is eternal
this *Summer* wants to stain everything in her path in this glow.

NO ONE IS LOOKING, I PROMISE

You are most yourself when you are bleeding,
when you are trying to keep your tongue from
falling out. When you are relearning the language that
once turned you into a ghost. You are most yourself in therapy,
or outside of therapy—as long as you are talking to someone
about something. As long as you keep your guts from spilling
out. You are most yourself with your sadness stapled to your chest,
when the birds are screaming, when the princess
dies at the end of the movie—alone and ugly. It reminds you
that not everything turns out
good, that not everyone smiles with a
mouth full of teeth. You are
most yourself at the end of the night,
when you shower off your grief
and put on a fresh coat. You were most yourself
five years ago, before your memories grew limbs
and crawled out of your childhood home. You
are most yourself right now, at the end of this poem:
as the sky bruises like you've never seen it.

CHANT

I find myself choking on a body of water.
I find myself choking on a body.
I find myself choking on my body.
I find myself choking.
I find myself—
then lose her again.

I unhinge my mechanical jaw.

       [I've knitted through this grief and now it's a noose.]

It did nothing to stop me from burning.

       [I've knitted through this grief and now it's a noose.]

I was once a girl with milk teeth now I chew through all the walls.

       [I've knitted through this grief and now it's a noose.]

If a boy drowns but cannot sink; we call it a mirror.

       [I've knitted through this grief and now it's a noose.]

No one has ever had the pleasure of knowing me.

       [I've knitted through this grief and now it's a noose.]

No one has had the displeasure of keeping me.

       [I've knitted through this grief and now it's a noose.]

DARK CHOCOLATE

How dare you walk in here
and treat me like a fetish?
The audacity of you to
show up here when your sweet tooth throbs.
I am not a slab of chocolate
to melt under your tongue.
Do not come here expecting dessert.
I may speak English like the best of them
and abandon my mother-tongue at the
bottom of my throat to make it easier for you
to understand me, but do not mistake this
generosity for what it is not.
You come here trying to make a meal out of me?
I will eat you alive.

IF THIS WAS THE LAST THING I EVER WROTE

I want you to know that this was not how I wanted the words to come. I can't seem to deconstruct my traumas. I make no apologies for how I chose to swallow this wretchedness,
how I gave my body back to myself and deemed it to be gorgeous again. Do you even know what it took to stop the house from burning? What the smoke did to the rotting memories I kept locked in the basement? So I gave myself something to bury, something to write about, something to give a name to and call mine. I wanted an ache that was familiar. I stuffed metaphors underneath my tongue because I can't afford to spit out the past. And now that the world is ablaze and I have to morph into the thing that needs burying. Now that you have to write about me and give me a name and call me yours: make no apologies for how you choose to stop me from burning.

THE BLACK GIRL DIES IN THIS ONE

She always does.
Has gender shoved down her throat and then blamed for the gagging,
blamed for all the grief she coughs up.
If she won't wear this trauma like a noose, then she has picked the
wrong size of brown girl suffering.
If she isn't shaped like an hourglass,
then how will she know when her time is up?
Black girl is ticking with untapped rage—about how
her worth is reduced to a BLM highlight on an Instagram page,
about how each Pinterest board that has her skin as an aesthetic
is just another nail in her coffin,
or her cross,
or whatever else they will choose to bury her in.
Black girl has dreams beyond surviving despite the
bloodshed, but she cannot wake up from a nightmare she was born into.
If she is always trying to unlearn this rage around the clock
how will she know when her time is up?
Her time is up.

FOR GIRLS WITH DIFFICULT NAMES

Don't let your name slip through the fingers of
the wrong people like refined sand.
A time will come when the right person cradles
your name in their palms like soft clay
and finally;
molds it in your image.

MY ANXIETY KEEPS TELLING ME THAT EVERYONE I LOVE IS DEAD

my anxiety has knees, so it kneels at the foot
of my bed until i open the covers to let it in.
suddenly my blood has run cold.
suddenly the hill is a bloody mountain.
suddenly my body is a multiple-choice exam and none
of the answers are the right one.
everyone i love is dead even though
they're right here. everyone i love is dead even though
they reassure me they're not.
my anxiety has plans so it kisses me goodbye for now.
and suddenly everyone i love is not dead, but they
will be someday.
my blood runs cold.

PROMISES, PROMISES

Someday I will love someone without ever having to write about it. And when this happens, I will call them first. We will laugh about nothing in particular and make plans for a future without blood and it will be magnificent. I will hang up without saying goodbye and my hands will tremble like an addict desperate for a fix except the fix is a life well-lived and the addict is me with a pen. But I won't write about it. I won't create a half-hearted metaphor about this full-hearted feeling. Instead, I will love you—mid-sentence—and uninterrupted.

Anything can seem like a threat if you're victim
enough. The friendly man in the store—threat.
Your ex who says he didn't hear you say no—a threat.
Suddenly your body belongs to anyone who calls *dibs* in
their head. Your hands are an invitation. Your
mouth is an ornament. Your voice is in your
pocket for safekeeping. Nobody believes you.
Nobody understands that just because you
didn't say something when it
happened doesn't mean it *didn't* happen.
Nobody understands that there is protest
in silence, too.

HOUSE HUNTING

For this bullet loved the child of soil so much that it
made a ~~hole~~ home in the spaces between tissue and skin.
Missed the heart by a millimeter but still kissed it on the way in.
It cocooned inside a brown body and made furniture out of the
rubble left behind. It thought nothing of the wreckage because
that's what made it such a beautiful dwelling.
The ~~body~~ house embraces the ground with all the vigor of a
thing that is used to kneeling,
used to being buried.
The bullet thinks nothing of where it came from.
It has already forgotten the hands that evicted it from its
metal cage but it's thankful to be here: to open the gates so that
the ~~blood~~ flood dries up.
And when the tiresome noise of gasping and choking finally stops,
when the house stops creaking and jerking and becomes motionless
and still like all good homes are; the bullet turns off the light and finally
falls asleep.

AFFIRMATIONS FOR THE AVERAGE BLACK GIRL

I am worthy. *Until literally everyone decides that I'm not.*

I deserve a good life. *One that I can carve out myself.*

I will not cry when a steaming bowl of bullets is emptied into another black belly.

I am more than enough. *Which is why everyone keeps taking pieces of me without asking.*

I love myself. I love myself. I love myself. *The repetition helps.*

Nothing can hurt me if I don't let it. *Except I know the smell of my own blood.*

THE GROCERY STORE KNOWS ALL HER SECRETS

No one knows that the girl in aisle 6 squeezing the avocado to assess its ripeness has lost the war today. She is checking the firmness, but she is shaking. She is shaking and no one notices. A baby in a trolley cries and she empathizes. And perhaps it's incorrect to compare herself to a baby but she did need protecting. She did need soothing, needed someone's finger to grip and a guarantee that she won't remember this phase of her life in five years. But she will. There is no way one can forget an unbecoming like this. She is unraveling in the middle of aisle 6 and no one is batting an eye. There is an ache in her marrow and her stem cells keep making copies. Maybe one day she won't be so ripe   for the taking.

MY HEART AND OTHER DEAD THINGS

You'd think the sound of your heart breaking would be an earth-shattering
disaster—
but really, it's the softest thing: how it just cracks
without warning. And suddenly the silence is all you can hear
because this wretched thing has finally stopped beating. But you still have the
rest of your body—and it's waiting for you to love it.
And sometimes sadness feels like the only thing that fits me anymore.
And I'm holding off on buying anything new because I want to believe that I
can still wear emotions from years ago. But everything is snug—everything is
suffocating.
There is nothing that leaves you feeling quite so small as
carrying all of this grief in your palms.

A WINDOW INTO THIS FEELING

Everything about this grief is my own. Its sharp teeth—mine. The sweltering heat that comes with it—also mine. Everything about this grief is my own except the calamities that cause it.

Have you ever had misery laced into your wrist? Had it glow under the weight of a clasped hand? I have been made terrifying: festering each time I look in the mirror and find a new way to hurt myself.

I can name it *shame* or *misery*, or a brief pause in what others might call joy. All I know is it's mine and I wear it well.

THAT PIT IN YOUR STOMACH IS JUST THE HOLE I CARVED WHEN I LEFT.

The word you're looking for is regret.
There are things you regret and
there are things that regret you.
They mean the same thing if you squint hard enough.
You, with all those nerve endings and
unfinished stories,
have the audacity to be one more false truth
away from being an erased memory.
I like to think you would say my name when someone asks you about the one
that got away.
I hope you tell them about how you woke up one morning to discover I was
gone,
almost as if I was never really there,
leaving behind only the realization,
that I finally did it:
I finally left.

You knew about all the ghosts that I have loved,
and you still decided to haunt me.

HEIRLOOMS

In every room I enter
I see three of my ancestors seated in chairs.
They do not age but there is nothing young about the look in their eyes.
I ask them the same question each time.
How am I meant to love?

My great-great-grandmother goes first:
*You love the one who hurts you the least. The scars should fade by the time you
notice them.*

My great-grandmother is next:
*You love the one who hurts you the most. Love without pain is just diluted
affection.*

Finally, my grandmother:
*Love the one who hurts you but apologizes for it in the morning. Feed on their
remorse like fermented fruit.*

What if I want a love that doesn't hurt? I ask.
They laugh,
then smile.
It doesn't reach their eyes.

THERE WAS A LYNCHING ON MY BIRTHDAY

a rope does its own form of dancing I suppose.
it does wrap its arms around a pulsing neck
Sweeps a body off its feet

                    Clutches breath.

imagine the artistry of brown silhouettes under a tree
gyrating then

                            stillness.

I keep making poetry out of my kin's death because if history has taught me
anything it's

It doesn't matter how ugly it looks; it will resurrect itself in things that provoke
ruin. My brother loves to dance.
I press my palms to my pulsing neck and

                    clutch my breath.

AUTOPSY

Father says I need to exist beyond that moment.
He says,
The time has passed for me to weep.

He says,
"Time waits for no one, baby girl. Dust it off."

So, I do.
I spit out the blood pooling in my mouth.
I pick my liver up from off the floor and polish it.
My lungs come next: I rinse off the mud and cigarette smoke.
I find my kidneys at the bottom of the ocean; pickled by salt.
The pancreas didn't have time to escape.
My heart couldn't have gone far.
I shove my organs back inside and stitch myself back together.
I do not ask for help.
I do not need it.

"Good," Father says. "Don't you ever fall apart like that again."

I used to be so good at finding your hand in a crowded room. Now everything is a ghost town.

DREAM GIRL

It was going so well until you had to go and ruin it by calling me your dream girl. I am not meant to be a dream, something you have to close your eyes to see only to wake up screaming because this is not what you envisioned me to be. I don't know how to love you and mean it. And by that, I mean a clean love unsullied by my tarnished palms. You, my love, are soft clay and I will mold you until you harden and crack. This is a really long way to say I will break you and leave you jaded. I am not your breath of fresh air, not your glass half full. Do not drink then spit me out as if I didn't warn you that this bitterness is all I know. I am not your dream. So, close your eyes. I'll watch your eyelids flicker and your breathing deepen and when you awake, I'll be gone. You tasted like the rest of my life. I just wasn't starving anymore.

PROMISE ME

you can go ahead and love someone else all you want—just don't love them the
way you loved me.

MEDUSA

despite all my efforts, you looked directly at me and turned into stone. you will
grow to love the things you damage. my first act as girl
was to obey.
i am hardly a villain but i do remember being more unblemished in my origin
story.
i should have known that you reeked of goneness when i met you.
i can usually spot a lost cause from a mile away, but i wanted so desperately to
belong to anyone that i mistook the flashing neon sign about your head for a
halo.
forgive me; sometimes my hunger catches me off guard.
and if we can't be together then let's at least have a bloodless ending?
i want to watch you quietly leave and not have you look so familiar.
i want to hold the door open as you do.

ANTAGONIST

He entered the room like a punished memory—this is how most of my dreams begin.

Without saying a word, he becomes both the knife and the balm, both the wolf and the boy who cried. It's for this reason that no one believes me when I say I can't tell the difference between that which wants to consume me from that which wants to swallow me whole. How can he be so young and carry centuries of bloodshed beneath his ribs? His footsteps sound vaguely familiar—where have I heard that sound before? Is it the sharpening of a knife? The rumble of his laughter? I cannot seem to tell the difference anymore.

SCAPEGOAT

You're not always blameless. Sometimes you speak. Sometimes you leave the
house. Sometimes you say no and mean it. Each time you get uglier. Each time
the audience boos you off the stage. Nothing about you is sacred. Everyone
says your name like it isn't blasphemy. You've rotted to the core and the world
assumes it's your natural scent. You're not guiltless, sometimes you breathe.

BLACK GIRL MAGIC

turning rage into silence// a prayer into a lost cause // this skin into a mounted
painting // have a heart fat with loss and still give // sing with a mouth full
of language that is not my own // mourn the language stolen from me //
abracadabra myself a new smile // disappear with the snap of a finger // return
to rubble and start from scratch // to be cut in half // to be a black daughter //
an exotic friend // an obsidian sister // a dark skin wife // belong to anything
but myself // there is not a potion that can unskin me // unwoman me // undo
me // there is nothing that masks this holy // they're calling this // witchcraft

Has no one ever told you that the only difference between girl and ghost is which room she chooses to haunt you in?

JUST ONE OF THE BOYS

I mean, I'm just like you. I mean, just as strong as you. I mean, I watch you rate girls on a scale of one to doable and I don't gouge out your eyes. I let you follow me home to protect me from monsters and we both act like it's not you. I grow out all my hair because it doesn't matter. I wear hoodies around you. I don't try and be desirable for you. I don't attempt to please you, and you pretend this doesn't make you angry. Because I'm one of the boys. Because I'm one of the things you finally find human.

BE A LANDING

Let the record show that I tried.
I waved the white flag and surrendered. I volunteered as tribute. I carved the
scarlet letter on my forehead with my own blood. It did nothing to fix my
crooked guilt.
You hunted my feelings for sport and ate the carcass for dinner.
You renamed each fermented memory of us so you could
watch them when no one was looking. To live as this wretched thing is
to write poems for all the things my
tongue was too thick to say in person.
You wanted so desperately to be somebody else, so if you must be something,
then be a landing.

LANGUAGE

He told me the weirdest thing about him was that he liked words with a silent
"d".
As in, he lived on the *edge*. As in, he was born on a *Wednesday* so he's full of
woe
or something. As in, I *pledged* allegiance to the veins on his hands
so many times. As in, who am I to *judge* how someone deals with the ache?
He thought it was so weird, but I thought it was the best thing about him.
I could find joy in watching paint dry if I was doing it with him.
But then he said *I love(d) you*,
but forgot to tell me that the d was silent.

POST-WAR

All jokes aside, it doesn't hurt anymore. I'm serious. I won't call you. I won't even think about it. I will listen to sad songs and it will have nothing to do with you. My friends won't talk shit about you. I'll make them swear to remove your existence from their memory and only invoke your name in horror stories. I'll eat when I'm hungry—I still cannot believe I starved myself for you, anyways. I'm told love makes you do crazy things. I guess I went mad for good measure.

SYMMETRY

I live so far outside my body I didn't even notice when the knife began to twist.
I don't recognize all these new lesions and swellings.
I have outgrown my knees. They bump into all the furniture.
I cry—unprovoked. I dream of my not yet conceived daughter.
She doesn't have a face yet, but she is a door marked exit.
I have already failed her in a thousand ways.
I don't name her in my language because I don't want her to understand me.
I imagine myself screaming her name as she
walks out of the home I will give her.
I imagine she won't hear me call after her.
I imagine she'll take her good knees and a clean knife
and walk towards the rest of her body.

What if you didn't survive? What if what you call survival is just an act of rebellion?

SHRINKING

My aunt has this running joke that I was born hungry,
and she tells it at every family gathering. I always laugh.
Then starve myself for the next few days.
I know I take up too much space with this appetite for softer endings.
I try to love myself then I switch on the tv or my phone and the food vanishes from my
palms like an exhaled breath.
So I run and I run and I hope it will make me float
or be prettier or at the very least take me away from here.

THIS ISN'T FOR YOU (I THINK)

There is this person (not you, of course) who loves everything. It just can't be helped. They just can't seem to keep themselves warm enough to stay. It's a constant ache and it's hard to breathe, sometimes. But they wake up each morning and put on their normal clothes and their normal smiles and go to their normal jobs like they weren't weapons the night before. This person lives through the ringing in their ears until a violent ending is inevitable. But this is just a random person. This has nothing to do with you.

PRETTY FOR A BLACK GIRL

A gorgeous little thing, you are.
A maze of dark skin that leads men to sin.
You look good enough to eat
Good enough to swallow whole
Good enough to spit out
Imagine how much prettier you would be
with an accent
With straight hair
With a softer voice
Imagine how good you could look
in a body bag.

AUTOPSY II

in my seventh rotation around the sun, the boy in my second-grade class calls
me ugly and i just internalized it. and every subsequent year since, i rip out the
stitches in my abdomen, pull out my organs and count each abnormality. my
heart gains a new blemish each month and it's all my fault because i'm a sucker
for brown eyes and a nice smile. my lungs deflate with each panic attack that
lasts more than the length of my favorite song. i perform annual surgery on
myself because i don't trust doctors to not leave anything foreign in me—like
love and self-acceptance. i wilt under the gaze of every person who has called
me beautiful. i wait for the punchline, for the *just kidding*.
in my twentieth rotation around the sun, the girl in my neuroanatomy class
calls me beautiful and i call her a liar. the neat, surgical scar on my lower
abdominal begins to throb.

all I wanted was to be loved and you made it seem like it was this impossible, miserable thing.

I SEE THIS GIRL CRY ON HER INSTAGRAM STORIES

And I think I must be mad because I've
seen this before. I, too, have sobbed in front of witnesses.
They too, have swiped past it.

THERE MIGHT BE HOPE; AFTER ALL

The body takes on the shape of a grief-sized envelope. Folds unwillingly to the size of a rectangle but never touches the corners of healing. I tell my therapist that I don't feel like dying today and that's good enough for me. It's good enough that I still want my hands. It's good enough that I use them to feel when my mind takes a local anesthetic. I call myself weak for pouring myself into today. I call myself stupid for thinking tomorrow could be different: that I would wake up with the sun on my face and I would bask in it. But all it does is remind me that the world keeps spinning, that it keeps discovering itself in a new light. All it does is paint my misery orange. I want this even if it destroys me: I want this especially then.

PHARMACY

If memory serves me well, the boy
who has my heart keeps it locked
in his medicine cabinet, between
his chronic pain meds and anti-
depressants. As he pops the pills
into the oasis of his mouth every
morning, he gives my beating organ
a squeeze, as if to say, *at least we're
both getting help. At least this room
is still bloodless.*

How do I say I don't want to be owned but I desperately want to belong to someone, without sounding like a lost cause?

DELIRIUM

You've always confused love for a whale—the way it swallows you whole and keeps you in its belly. Every morning, you try to gnaw yourself free. Every evening, you accept your fate. Without fail, people have made your tenderness an ugly thing. Treated it like a crime. It's why you've grown to believe you're a danger to everything with a steady pulse. You take nothing for granted, especially the people who touch you with clean hands. You confuse everything for love, including hunger.

HYPOTHETICALLY, OF COURSE.

So for the purposes of this poem let's say I am loved.
Let's say you can see it on my face.
Like, yes someone wants her.
Can't you see? She glows.
There's no question about it.
Let's say my nightmares don't have hands, that they don't grip me by the
throat. Perhaps my abuser didn't call me a week after he was released.
Let's say I didn't lock myself in my room for a week afterwards.
In what alternate reality do I undo all this damage?
Which version of me can recognize a good thing when it's handed to me?
Let's say I know what it means to survive beyond tonight.
What would that even look like? How do I stop the stinging bite beneath my
eyelids? How do I even adequately explain myself to you?
But these are just words.
Let's just say they don't mean anything.

THINGS I WISH I SAID (BUT NEVER DID)

1. That rape/black/sexist joke wasn't funny, nor was it a joke. I refuse to let you laugh at my expense. There's the exit.
2. The architecture of my body is a well-kept secret. I only tell it to those who leave their shoes at the door.
3. I hate the way Nutella tastes. It's weird and sweet and I would burn the world down before I put it in my mouth.
4. I like to be alone, but I don't want to be lonely.
5. There are some people I wish I never met. But I still invite them over for dinner.
6. I, too, am capable of becoming a subject of someone else's ache.
7. I love you.
8. I love you.
9. I love you.
10. I repeat things when I'm lying.

A POEM IN WHICH I REPLACE THE WORD BITCH WITH SISTER BECAUSE THE ONLY TIME MEN RESPECT WOMEN IS WHEN THEY'RE ATTRACTED OR RELATED TO THEM.

This sister does what she wants with her body because it belongs to her and her alone. This sister doesn't flinch when the men follow her home because it is the third time today and if she runs, they will mistake her for prey, so she walks slow and prays that her mother won't see her on the 6 o' clock news. This sister is covered in hijab. This sister is showing some ankle. This sister is showing her belly and her arms, and it makes no difference to them because the issue is not what she is wearing, it's just that she is there for the taking. This sister sometimes wants to be called brother or just sibling because labels matter to her and should be respected. This sister is tired of being looked at, gazed upon, perceived. This sister is tired of having her dignity come with strings attached.

HOW LOVELY IT IS TO BE BLACK

In theory.
On social media.
In white men's fantasies.
Everywhere
but real life.
Everywhere but here.
To exist in every space
and know you can be killed in
any of them.
Can we for a moment pretend that
this all ends well?
That one can be brown and
not have it mean anything other
than glowing in the sun.
God, how I wish I could bask in the sun
again.

THE NEXT WAR IS GOING TO KILL US ALL

and it won't be massive.
there won't be men in trenches with some misplaced sense of duty.
the news won't report it.
some of us will barely know it's happening.
we will be too busy making plans for the day after
next we will barely realize that we are fighting with
ourselves and we are losing.
we are losing and there's nothing we can do about it but
write our own eulogies in case everyone we love is too tired
to utter our names out loud anymore.
we will say, *I lived my life the best way I knew how.*
I'm sorry I regretted it in the end.

GENTRIFIED

Every girl of color I know is a half-erased mistake waiting to happen. We have the savagery of our languages snatched from our throats and plated at some gentrified restaurant. Our origin stories are the first time a white man finds us desirable and saves us from our third world countries and makes us take off cultures at the door. He saves us from the ghetto or the hijab or the cruelty of our native tongue.

We are mothered by a colonizer's need to save us from ourselves. The geography of our bodies is dissected and hung up in museums that call us uncivilized but fail to point out the places that slave ships sank. Even now, the white boy in my class tells me I'd be so much prettier if I smiled more. So I bare my teeth to remind him that a starving animal will sink its teeth into the first poacher that threatens its survival.

INSOMNIA

I don't sleep. Ever.
I don't ever close my eyes.
I don't breathe.
I never relax.
My jaw remains clenched.
I hyperventilate.
I vibrate with weird energy.
I forget my name (but never yours, never ever yours).
I drag my corpse out of the river.
I don't try to resuscitate it.
I laugh. Really loudly. It sounds hollow.
I move my limbs when I remember.
I place one foot in front of the other.
I walk.
I walk.
I walk.
I'm in the front of your house.
I don't knock.
I don't move.
I regurgitate the lies.
I dig my heels into the ground.
The vultures are picking at my carcass.
I try to close my eyes.
The memories slap me awake.
I'm so naive. I'm so stupid.
I deserve nothing,
not even a hand.
But I'm here.
I'm here.
I'm here.
I'm here.

[BLANK]

My therapist thinks I can't say the word love out loud
because the gravity of what it means terrifies me.
She says,
it's just four letters.
She says,
it can mean everything I want.
So, I try. I place my tongue to the roof of my mouth
and say love, but your name comes out instead.
Your name,
also four letters.
Your name,
everything I want.

FUN FACTS ABOUT THE HUMAN BODY

1. The average person's heart beats about 100,000 times a day.
    Your heart is about double that. You are a chest burdened by all that grit
    and mass, it's a wonder how you keep yourself afloat.
2. Humans are the only animals with chins. You are the only animal with
    soft teeth.
    It doesn't bode well at night.
3. Bones are about 5 times stronger than steel. Yet you crumble at the
    thought of me.
    You transform into an ocean of grief whenever you think of me.
4. Stomach acid can dissolve metal. If it touched your skin, it would burn
    right through it.
    If I touched your skin, I would burn right through it.

WHITE ACTIVIST EXPLAINS ERASURE TO ME

and I nod along as to not seem impolite.
Her hands are moving, and her face is animated as she explains my story. To me.
She adds BLM to her bio and absolves herself of guilt.
Tucks me in the corners of a hollowed-out book and pulls me out when she
needs to refresh her memory of this oppression.
From my black gums this story sounds
too much like an autobiography, like a dull throb history repeating itself.
In her delicate fingertips, this injustice is aesthetic.
She scribbles this black rage in a pretty font and receives an overwhelming
applause.
Gets a standing ovation off the backs of my ancestors. Accepts the award on my
behalf.
She says she's sorry for all that I have to go through. Uses that pink tongue of
hers to soothe the sting of my silence.
Her work here is done.

MY HISTORY TEACHER SPENDS MONTHS TEACHING ME ABOUT APARTHEID

Would you mind terribly if I started a war?
Not a huge one.
Maybe one with a few dead bodies on either side.
We would have a memorial.
We would teach this war in history class but change a few minor details.
And every year, on the anniversary of what was once heroes in trenches,
we would raise the flag.
Any flag—as long as it represents surrender.
A classroom full of children will be taught about a white man who
knocked on their country's door and walked in—uninvited.
We will name a street after him.
We will vow to never let it happen again.
We will pretend we aren't lying.

BACK TO THE FUTURE 2

Ask the girl you love where she will be five years from now and she won't know. She barely knows what's for dinner tonight. She goes to school. Does well even. She's not a mess but makes chaos of everything. She wants a house. Wants to provide for her parents and her little sister. She just started going to therapy for her anxiety and depression but feels guilty about it, feels like she has no right to be this sad. She has a roof over her head and the world probably won't implode in her lifetime. She doesn't know if she wants kids but knows she would have to work at being a good mother. Because parenthood is work. There is no way that comes naturally—to anyone. The girl you love doesn't have a driver's license yet—not because she doesn't want one but every time she is in a car that's near a huge truck, she thinks it will crush her. The girl you love doesn't know you love her. She calls you her best friend and kisses your knuckles absent-mindedly. She doesn't make plans for the future but if she did, if she ever did, you would be a big part of it.

SILENCE

So, I'm studying for my anatomy final in the library when I get a text that reads: another one shot dead. It's not until someone shushes me that I realize I'm whimpering. So, I pack up the loudness of the dead girl's bones and leave to give everyone some quiet. It's not lost on me that I have had so many moments of silence for the deaths of every black boy and girl I dared to learn the name of. I've filled that silence with a closed fist pressed to the lips of a watery smile. I know by heart the wail of a mother's tongue when she discovers her daughter's name is the number one thing trending: her pretty face nailed to every palm that has had the pleasure of feeling her pulse. We place flowers at her memorial site as if we're not placing dead things at another dead thing. We say their names until our voices crack all over the asphalt their bodies were found on but still no one hears us.

MY MOTHER IS A BETTER POET THAN ME

At dinner, my mother tells me for the 100th time the story of my birth, about how her body stretched to welcome me and how the splitting of her anatomy only made her more whole. She describes our bond as the most beautiful math problem; says even though her hips had to divide and crack under the weight of my arrival, her joy multiplied at seeing my bloody face when the nurse placed me on her chest.

My mother doesn't cry; she floats on a bed of tears. She doesn't laugh; she pierces the air with a cackle so loud and foreign you can't help but laugh with her. Her anger knows no boundaries; it travels far and wide and burns anything that dares to tell her to calm down.

A little while ago; I bashfully showed her a picture of the boy I like, and she told me how she liked that his mouth looked like it was in quotation marks. It took me a minute to realize she was talking about his dimples.

WE ARE OWED

a semblance of dignity
the chance to outlive a bullet
the chance to outrun our abusers.
a reality to be dark, beautiful, and alive.
bodies that don't remember an unwanted
touch, broken bones or fading bruises.
a bus ride that doesn't end with a pale hand
in our hair.
strangers that don't call us niggers
friends that don't call us niggers
to be mothered
to not die at our own hands
an apology
an, *I'm sorry*
a, *we cannot begin to imagine what it's like to be black and*
woman and be owed.

BLACKOUT POEM OF THE TEXT FROM A GUY I GHOSTED FOR NO REASON OTHER THAN A MAJOR DEPRESSIVE EPISODE (I'M SORRY)

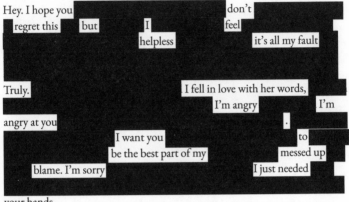

Hey. I hope you don't
regret this but I feel
helpless it's all my fault

Truly. I fell in love with her words,
I'm angry I'm
angry at you .
I want you to
be the best part of my messed up
blame. I'm sorry I just needed

your hands.

BONDAGE

I used to think I knew so much about what love was supposed to
feel like until he let go of my hand one afternoon.
He said it was because his palms were sweaty but
I knew better. You don't love something then set it free—whoever
came up with that phrase didn't know what they were talking about.
You love something and keep it, until it thrashes out of your grasp
and into new chains. He let go of my hand that afternoon and
never held it again. Now the next hand I hold will be nothing but me,
just passing the time.
I will grip this new, sweaty hand but
I will not call it love, just in case it is captivity
this whole time.

Some days you are the light; other days you are the switch.

girlhood is having your father rewrite your life and forgetting to tell you about it.

BOOKMARK

don't rock the boat. don't breathe too loud
or make any sudden movements. don't be an air balloon—stop placing people
into your body and giving them the right to float at your own peril. everything
you have ever known is blunt force trauma. the bruising of your arm can be
anything you want, believe me.
the boy you love can be your father if he abandons you soon enough. life can
be so simple—just say the word. just say the word and we can rearrange a new
ending for you. don't rock the boat. the world could crack in two
if you even try to be anything other than a placeholder.

SUNDANCE FILM FESTIVAL

The movie opens with a fight scene: this couple in the middle of their living room.

We can't tell how long they have been together but in the back of the room there's a blurry photo frame. The flowers on the table are wilting. The cushions on the couch are different shades of green. These things are all deliberate. We'd like to imagine that it's mid-afternoon (there's a lot of natural lighting). The woman paces around the table. The man runs his hands through his hair. They're both frustrated and they're both angry. This much we can tell. This much we can decipher from the screen. The woman says something about wasting her youth. Her husband/boyfriend/significant other replies that it's not his fault. This goes on for several minutes. There are flashbacks and a violin concerto to add to the dramatic tension and we eat it up. We secretly pray for their downfall. It's been 20 minutes and they have done nothing but go to war. A bunch of other things happen in the movie, but we do not care about that. We're still thinking about the fight scene. We're thinking about how the woman screams "YOU HAVE NEVER BLED FOR ME!" and how the man tiredly points to his woundless body and says: "What do you think I'm doing now? Isn't this a type of bleeding?"

yes, what you're going through is unbearable
and it's heavy and it makes you want to
scream all the goddamn time
but you're still here and it's still bearable *because*
you're still bearing it and it's so
colossally heavy but you're still carrying it
so fill your lungs with all
that deserved rage and scream.

what an unfortunate situation: you wanted
to love me
but all it did was remind me
that i was once an unloved experience.

NOAH DOESN'T TALK ABOUT HIS MOTHER ANYMORE.

In every definition of grief, he found himself walking back home. The porch doesn't creak, and the dog doesn't bark but there is a light in the kitchen. His mother, all the right shades of brown, is making jollof rice and the heady aroma finds him outside. He doesn't go into the house. He is content with listening to her melodic voice sing ancient hymns. His mother named him after his father, in the hopes that he would survive in ways his father never could. He has never had aggression beaten into him, so he knows how to hold something with the tenderness it requires. There is somebody he loves but he is not sure he is supposed to. And in between the porch creaking and the dog not barking, he realizes his mother is no longer here. The aroma he smells is just the memory of her bones. If you look closely, the house begins to shrink.

Why do I keep singing the same
song; why does it sound different
depending on the size of the injury?
Why can't I hear those birds
anymore? What has become
of the dead? Why do I keep them
tucked in my second mouth? Why
do I speak so many languages,
Who taught me this cruel dialect?
In a dream, I am still a child
with a fever that won't break.
In reality, I am still a child
but the fever is a welcomed
parasite. Language changes
depending on the bloodstain.

When you traced constellations on the back of my hand with the orbit of your fingers, I decided right then and there that I would shatter into a million stars on the blank canvas of night because it meant I would fall for you whenever you made a wish.

DESCRIBING MY EARLY TWENTIES USING THE ALPHABET.

Adolescent mimicry.
Burning Bush.
Clean wound.
Damaged Goods.
Embarrassingly difficult.
Forgiving.
Gone.
Hostility at its finest.
Initiation into the Unknown.
Jumping through hoops.
Kindling.
Licking wounds.
Miracle (I have made it this far).
New Language.
Obstacle Course.
Panic Attacks.
Quiet (Gaping).
Rust.
Stained Mirrors.
Ticking Time Bomb.
Unforgiving.
Volatile.
Weapon of Mass Destruction.
E(x)istential Crisis.
You.
Zoomed-in Polaroids of my best moments.

BLACK GIRL LOSES HER TEMPER

she's already lost everything else
what's one more thing.
the brown girl loses her temper
and she has never looked more beautiful.
you must understand,
ethnic girls inherit rage, and it simmers
it boils beneath their skin,
almost cut their tongues on the bitterness
because that bitch and that angry black girl
know all too well that it's better to be thought of as angry than to be seen as
afraid.
the last time a black girl was terrified,
they gave her something to
cry about.

A CASE STUDY ON WAYS TO SURVIVE.

1. Bleed on everything: on the concrete. In the middle of a fancy restaurant.
    In the car on the way to work. Bleed and bleed and bleed until someone
    follows the trail and finally believes you.
2. Assume that everyone you meet has boomerangs for hands, that at some
    point they will come back and hold you.
3. Remove your heart from your sleeve and staple it to your forehead. Maybe
    that way, someone will notice it.
4. Take your meds. Pretend they're candy. Have them melt on your tongue
    while the light dims. It's not supposed to hurt. Any of it.
5. Use your mouth for good. Kiss your friends. Call a stranger beautiful.
    Mold your tongue around a prayer and plead for a better day.

THE TRIALS AND TRIBULATIONS OF HAVING FREQUENT PANIC ATTACKS DURING BLACK HISTORY MONTH.

none of my kin were born by a river but you can be certain that our blood
taints the waters. the absence of racism
is not safety or dignity—these are the
lessons our ancestors taught us.
my favorite sidewalk used to house a
bench that only white people could sit on—
this is the country i was born in.
i am always aware of my blackness
it doesn't give me a day off it
follows me everywhere it's a
lighthouse that slave ships follow
i can't catch my breath in any retail
store the employees follow me
down the aisle the white woman
in the grocery store touches my hair in the frozen goods
section and i smile at her instead of
ripping her arm off—these are the comforts i give to micro aggressions.
there is a bullet somewhere with
my name on it and the hardest
part is the waiting.

PRAISE KINK

call me beautiful.
call me a good girl.
say i have mastered daughterhood.
pat my head
watch me pant under a woundless sky.
give a collar with your initials on it.
say that you own me,
that i belong to something other than this.
tell me i am doing a good job keeping my body from finding gentler borders.
tell me i deserve what's coming, that if i
valued myself a little bit more, i might
have had a different fate.
but these are the chains i have got.
they don't chafe my wrists as badly as
i thought they would.
i would have done anything you said.
i would have walked through the proverbial fire.
call me beautiful,
i beg of you.

IN WHICH THE SPEAKER IS SPEAKING TO NO ONE OTHER THAN HERSELF

I'll give you until the end of this poem to decide:
have you ever disintegrated in the middle of your childhood home?
Did you put your body back together in a hurry and now nothing feels quite
right anymore?
I don't know much about anything, but I know you are beautiful in the way
the sky is blue and apples are fruit—it's just a fact of life. But you cry a little
too hard at sad movies and you hate having candles on your birthday cake. You
don't even know why.
Did you give it your best shot? I'm not sure you really even tried.
I know I can be difficult. I think it has to do with the way my brain is wired or
that unspeakable night I turned fifteen and doubled as a crime scene.
Somewhere along the way, I lost my mind and I've been making do
with the tools I have left but at least I *tried*.
I held your hand. I forgave you almost instantly.
But you made your monsters mine and suddenly I was the
cracked mirror you checked your reflection in.
I helped you stitch your heart back together once.
Do you even remember?

ALL ANIMALS ARE EQUAL; BUT SOME ANIMALS ARE MORE EQUAL THAN OTHERS.

There are rich men in space and hundreds of
Palestinian bodies all over the blackened earth and
we act like this is normal
like this is not
insanity
that people can be so greedy that all
they have is money and all it does is make them
greedier. There are rich men in space and starving
children all over the blackened earth
their ribcages have nowhere to hide, and we feed them
lies and feed them false hope and say things like
if you work hard enough one day you will earn
barely enough to die in a borrowed home and not
on the pavement like all the other peasants who
don't get to go to
space.

It is terrifying to wonder whether the person you love is a walking red flag or a white flag of surrender dipped in your own blood. You have already dusted the cobwebs in your heart to make space for them. What are you meant to do with all this room you've made? *Love yourself instead.*

THE HANDS KEEP SCORE

of everything beautiful i have taken away from myself.
of every orange slice that kept my shaky fingers cool.
of the self-harm scars.
of every other hand that has showed it kindness or even
fury.
of every prayer mat they have touched in *sajdah*.
of every body they have hugged and sacrificed warmth to.
of the memory of every fading bruise that gave them a
different shade of blue.
of every new language they expressed when my tongue felt
too heavy in my mouth,
of every song
of every name
of every lifetime that has you in it.

The last person I adored made me cry and then tenderly wiped the tears off my face. It was the only lesson he ever taught me: you can love someone and still do horrible, cruel things to them.

CONFESSIONS IV

Here's the thing. Gun to my head? I would choose
you again. Maybe. I'm not sure anymore. But you
used to call me *angel* and I swear it made me
levitate. You used to call me. Full stop. Now we're
strangers with only a cancerous past keeping us
tethered together. Gun to head? I would have held
the house together, brick by brick. Your
recollection of me wouldn't be so
pixelated. We would go on our daily run (well, your daily run,
my daily walk) and that would be our life. I would have
forgiven you for everything and anything. And
that's the problem. Because even now, there's a
hypothetical gun to my head and I can't help but
think: the bullet might hurt less.

SYMPTOMS OF WOMANHOOD

According to science, I should live to be at least 80.
According to memory, I'll be dead whenever he sees fit.

My love language is saying no and having him listen to me.

My mother hands me a first aid kit on my sixteenth birthday
because some wounds you have to heal yourself.

My little brother whistles at a young girl as he walks down
the street and I am reminded that even the men we love can
be dangerous.

I watch as my body is picked at and reduced to whatever
beauty standards are trending this week. I keep shrinking
under the harsh light of a gaze that does not belong to me.
I count myself lucky when I wake in the morning and find
myself untouched or unharmed or alive. I count myself lucky
because there is a girl right now who cannot.

you can breathe, you know? you're allowed a
moment of peace. someone should hold your
hand. they don't get to call you a ghost and live
without the haunting. moonlight has touched your
skin over and over again and you act like that is
not a miracle. the world begins at the sound of
your name, believe me. you, my love, are like
coming up for air. no one taught you how to be
human but you do it so well. you are brimming
with the enormity of your mistakes and nothing
has ever been more beautiful. you are not a
monster: your teeth are supposed to be that
sharp. keep your anger tucked in your body:
unleash it on anyone who trespasses. be brutally
selfish. what will be left of you if you keep letting
others take? you are allowed to breathe, believe
me.

ACKNOWLEDGMENTS

I'd like to thank my mom and dad, who will likely never read this in its entirety (not because they don't want to, but because they see each poem engraved on my skin every time they look at me).

I'd also like to thank my friends: Meghan, Adjo, Afroze, Josie, Zah'raa & Codi. They've seen this book when it was just a mess of words and loved it anyway.

A big thank you to my siblings/cousins/family—I'm so thankful we share blood.

And of course, a huge thank you to Michelle and the Central Avenue team for taking a chance on me and making this entire process so much easier. I'm forever grateful.

Sumaya Enyegue is a poet from Cape Town, South Africa, trying to navigate her early twenties while simultaneously juggling med school and spilling her feelings all over social media. When she isn't writing, you can find her reading, frantically trying to find her stethoscope, or pretending she's a functioning adult. Her favorite things include the color green, British panel shows, her family, her friends, and Captain Raymond Holt from B99.

instagram: @sumayapoetry
tiktok: sumayae

central
avenue
PUBLISHING

Central Avenue is a home for fiction and poetry about
us at our worst — and best.

We are proud to have had many of our titles on
bestseller lists, go viral, win respected awards, endorsed
by literary heroes and celebrities, and enjoyed by
readers all over the world.

Learn more about how this independent press works,
our books, and our authors at the link below.